C000016118

LOVE POEMS

ALSO AVAILABLE IN THIS FORMAT

The War Poets

William Wordsworth

Shakespeare Anthology

Shakespeare Birthday Book

Shakespeare Sonnets

Shakespeare Treasury

LOVE POEMS – AN ANTHOLOGY

Poems selected by Michael Wylie
Designed by Parke Sutton Publishing Limited
for Jarrold Publishing, Norwich
First published 1994. Reprinted 2000.

ISBN 0-7117-0678-6

Printed in China.

CONTENTS

SIR WILLIAM ALEXANDER,
EARL OF STIRLING

TO AURORA

I swear, Aurora, by thy starry eyes,
And by those golden locks whose lock none slips,
And by the coral of thy rosy lips,
And by the naked snows which beauty dyes,
I swear by all the jewels of thy mind,
Whose like yet never worldly treasure bought,
Thy solid judgement and thy generous thought,
Which in this darkened age have clearly shined:
I swear by those, and by my spotless love,
And by my secret yet most fervent fires,
That I have never nursed but chaste desires,
And such as modesty might well approve.
    Then since I love those virtuous parts in thee,
    Shouldst thou not love this virtuous mind in me?

O if thou knew'st how thou thyself dost harm,
And dost prejudge thy bliss, and spoil my rest;
Then thou would'st melt the ice out of thy breast
And thy relenting heart would kindly warm.
O if thy pride did not our joys control,

What world of loving wonders should'st thou see!
For if I saw thee once transform'd in me,
Then in thy bosom I would pour my soul;
Then all thy thoughts should in my visage shine,
And if that aught mischanced thou should'st not moan
Nor bear the burthen of thy griefs alone;
No, I would have my share in what were thine:
  And whilst we thus should make our sorrows one,
  This happy harmony would make them none.

ANONYMOUS

THE BAILIFF'S DAUGHTER OF ISLINGTON

There was a youth, and a well-belovèd youth,
And he was a squire's son:
He loved the bailiff's daughter dear,
That lived in Islington.

Yet she was coy, and would not believe
That he did love her so;
No, nor at any time would she
Any countenance to him show.

But when his friends did understand
His fond and foolish mind,
They sent him up to fair London,
An apprentice for to bind.

And when he had been seven long years,
And never his love could see:
"Many a tear have I shed for her sake,
When she little thought of me."

Then all the maids of Islington
Went forth to sport and play,
All but the bailiff's daughter dear;
She secretly stole away.

She pullèd off her gown of green,
And put on ragged attire,
And to fair London she would go
Her true love to inquire.

And as she went along the high road,
The weather being hot and dry,
She sat her down upon a green bank,
And her true love came riding by.

She started up with a colour so red,
Catching hold of his bridle-rein;
"One penny, one penny, kind sir," she said,
"Will ease me of much pain."

"Before I give you one penny, sweetheart,
Pray tell me where you were born."

"At Islington, kind sir," she said,
"Where I have had many a scorn."

"I prithee, sweetheart, then tell to me,
O tell me, whether you know
The bailiff's daughter of Islington."
"She is dead, sir, long ago."

"If she be dead, then take my horse,
My saddle and bridle also;
For I will unto some far country,
Where no man shall me know."

"O stay, O stay, thou goodly youth!
She standeth by thy side;
She is here alive, she is not dead,
And ready to be thy bride."

"O farewell grief and welcome joy,
Ten thousand times therefore!
For now I have found mine own true love,
Whom I thought I should never see more."

ANONYMOUS

LOVE WINGED MY HOPES

Love winged my hopes and taught me how to fly
Far from base earth, but not to mount too high:
  For true pleasure
  Lives in measure,
 Which, if men forsake,
Blinded they into folly run, and grief for pleasure take.

But my vain hopes, proud of their new-taught flight,
Enamoured sought to woo the sun's fair light,
  Whose rich brightness
  Moved their lightness
 To aspire so high,
That, all scorched and consumed with fire, now drowned in
 woe they lie.

And none but Love their woeful hap did rue;
For Love did know that their desires were true.
  Though Fate frownëd,
  And now drownëd
 They in sorrow dwell,
It was the purest light of heaven for whose fair love they fell.

Anonymous

My Lady Greensleeves

Alas! my love, you do me wrong
To cast me off discourteously;
And I have lovèd you so long,
Delighting in your company.
   Greensleeves was all my joy!
   Greensleeves was my delight!
   Greensleeves was my heart of gold!
   And who but my Lady Greensleeves!

I bought thee petticoats of the best,
The cloth so fine as fine as might be;
I gave thee jewels for thy chest,
And all this cost I spent on thee.
   Greensleeves, etc.

Thy smock of silk, both fair and white,
With gold embroidered gorgeously;
Thy petticoat of sendal right:
And these I bought thee gladly.
   Greensleeves, etc.

Thy gown was of the grassy green,
The sleeves of satin hanging by;
Which made thee be our harvest queen:
And yet thou wouldest not love me!
    Greensleeves, etc.

Greensleeves now farewell! adieu!
God I pray to prosper thee!
For I am still thy lover true:
Come once again and love me!
    Greensleeves was all my joy!
    Greensleeves was my delight!
    Greensleeves was my heart of gold!
    And who but my Lady Greensleeves!

Anonymous

What Remains But Only Dying?

Shall I look to ease my grief?
  No, my sight is lost with eyeing:
Shall I speak and beg relief?
  No, my voice is hoarse with crying:
  What remains but only dying?

Love and I of late did part,
  But the boy, my peace envying,
Like a Parthian threw his dart
  Backward, and did wound me flying:
  What remains but only dying?

She whom then I lookëd on,
  My remembrance beautifying,
Stays with me though I am gone,
  Gone and at her mercy lying:
  What remains but only dying?

Shall I try her thoughts and write?
  No, I have no means of trying:
If I should, yet at first sight

She would answer with denying:
   What remains but only dying?

Thus my vital breath doth waste,
   And, my blood with sorrow drying,
Sighs and tears make life to last
   For a while, their place supplying:
   What remains but only dying?

MATTHEW ARNOLD

THE FORSAKEN MERMAN

Come, dear children, let us away:
  Down and away below!
Now my brothers call from the bay;
  Now the great winds shoreward blow;
  Now the salt tides seaward flow;
Now the wild white horses play,
Champ and chafe and toss in the spray.
Children dear, let us away!
  This way, this way!

Call her once before you go.
  Call once yet.
In a voice that she will know:
  "Margaret! Margaret!"
Children's voices should be dear
(Call once more) to a mother's ear:
Children's voices, wild with pain –
Surely she will come again.
Call her once and come away;
  This way, this way!
"Mother dear, we cannot stay."

The wild white horses foam and fret.
  Margaret! Margaret!
Come, dear children, come away down!
    Call no more!
One last look at the white-walled town,
And the little grey church on the windy shore.
    Then come down.
She will not come though you call all day.
    Come away, come away!

Children dear, was it yesterday
We heard the sweet bells over the bay?
In the caverns where we lay,
Through the surf and through the swell,
The far-off sound of a silver bell?
Sand-strewn caverns, cool and deep,
Where the winds are all asleep;
Where the spent lights quiver and gleam;
Where the salt weed sways in the stream;
Were the sea-beasts ranged all round
Feed in the ooze of their pasture-ground;
Where the sea-snakes coil and twine,
Dry their mail and bask in the brine;
Where great whales come sailing by,

Sail and sail, with unshut eye,
Round the world for ever and ay?
When did music come this way?
Children dear, was it yesterday?

Children dear, was it yesterday
(Call yet once) that she went away?
Once she sate with you and me,
On a red gold throne in the heart of the sea,
And the youngest sate on her knee.
She comb'd its bright hair, and she tended it well,
When down swung the sound of the far-off bell.
She sigh'd, she look'd up through the clear green sea;
She said: "I must go, for my kinsfolk pray
In the little grey church on the shore to-day.
'Twill be Easter-time in the world — ah me!
And I lose my poor soul, Merman, here with thee."
I said: "Go up, dear heart, through the waves!
Say thy prayer, and come back to the kind sea-caves!"
She smiled, she went up through the surf in the bay.
Children dear, was it yesterday?

Children dear, were we long alone?
"The sea grows stormy, the little ones moan.

Long prayers," I said, "in the world they say.
Come!" I said, and we rose through the surf in the bay.
We went up the beach, by the sandy down
Where the sea-stocks bloom, to the white-walled town.
Through the narrow paved streets, where all was still,
To the little grey church on the windy hill.
From the church came a murmur of folk at their prayers,
But we stood without in the cold blowing airs.
We climbed on the graves, on the stones, worn with rains,
And we gazed up the aisle through the small-leaded
    panes.
She sate by the pillar; we saw her clear:
"Margaret, hist! come quick, we are here.
Dear heart," I said, "we are long alone.
The sea grows stormy, the little ones moan."
But, ah, she gave me never a look,
For her eyes were sealed to the holy book!
Loud prays the priest; shut stands the door.
Come away, children, call no more!
Come away, come down, call no more!

    Down, down, down!
    Down to the depths of the sea!
She sits at her wheel in the humming town,

Singing most joyfully.
Hark, what she sings: "O joy, O joy,
For the humming street, and the child with its toy!
For the priest, and the bell, and the holy well —
    For the wheel where I spun,
    And the blessed light of the sun!"
    And so she sings her fill,
    Singing most joyfully,
Till the shuttle falls from her hand,
    And the whizzing wheel stands still.
She steals to the window, and looks at the sand,
    And over the sand at the sea;
And her eyes are set in a stare;
    And anon there breaks a sigh,
And anon there drops a tear,
    From a sorrow-clouded eye,
And a heart sorrow-laden,
    A long, long sigh;
For the cold strange eyes of a little Mermaiden,
    And the gleam of her golden hair.

Come away, away children!
    Come children, come down!
The hoarse wind blows colder;

Lights shine in the town.
She will start from her slumber
　　When gusts shake the door;
She will hear the winds howling,
　　Will hear the waves roar.
We shall see, while above us
　　The waves roar and whirl,
A ceiling of amber,
　　A pavement of pearl.
Singing: "Here came a mortal,
　　But faithless was she!
And alone dwell for ever
　　The kings of the sea."

But children, at midnight,
　　When soft the winds blow,
When clear falls the moonlight,
　　When spring-tides are low;
When sweet airs come seaward
　　From heaths starred with broom,
And high rocks throw mildly
　　On the blanched sands a gloom;
Up the still, glistening beaches,
　　Up the creeks we will hie,

Over banks of bright seaweed
  The ebb-tide leaves dry.
We will gaze, from the sand-hills,
At the white, sleeping town;
At the church on the hill-side –
  And then come back down.
Singing: "There dwells a loved one,
  But cruel is she!
She left lonely for ever
  The kings of the sea."

SIR ROBERT AYTON

WHEN THOU DIDST THINK
I DID NOT LOVE

When thou didst think I did not love,
Then thou didst dote on me;
Now, when thou find'st that I do prove
As kind as kind can be,
   Love dies in thee.

What way to fire the mercury
Of thy inconstant mind?
Methinks it were good policy
For me to turn unkind,
   To make thee kind.

Yet will I not good nature strain
To buy, at so great cost,
That which, before I do obtain,
I make account almost
   That it is lost.

And though I might myself excuse
By imitating thee,
Yet will I no examples use
That may bewray in me
   Lightness to be.

But since I gave thee once my heart,
My constancy shall show
That though thou play the woman's part
And from a friend turn foe,
   Men do not so.

WILLIAM BLAKE

THE CLOD AND THE PEBBLE

"Love seeketh not Itself to please,
"Nor for itself hath any care,
"But for another gives its ease,
"And builds a Heaven in Hell's despair."

So sang a little Clod of Clay
Trodden with the cattle's feet,
But a Pebble of the brook
Warbled out these metres meet:

"Love seeketh only Self to please,
"To bind another to Its delight,
"Joys in another's loss of ease,
"And builds a Hell in Heaven's despite."

ROBERT BRIDGES

I WILL NOT LET THEE GO

I will not let thee go.
Ends all our month-long love in this?
  Can it be summed up so,
  Quit in a single kiss?
  I will not let thee go.

I will not let thee go.
If thy words' breath could scare thy deeds,
  As the soft south can blow
  And toss the feathered seeds,
  Then might I let thee go.

I will not let thee go.
Had not the great sun seen, I might;
  Or were he reckoned slow
  To bring the false to light,
  Then might I let thee go.

I will not let thee go.
The stars that crowd the summer skies
   Have watched us so below
   With all their million eyes,
   I dare not let thee go.

  I will not let thee go.
Have we not chid the changeful moon,
   Now rising late, and now
   Because she set too soon,
   And shall I let thee go?

  I will not let thee go.
Have not the young flowers been content,
   Plucked ere their buds could blow,
   To seal our sacrament?
   I cannot let thee go.

  I will not let thee go.
I hold thee by too many bands:
   Thou sayest farewell, and lo!
   I have thee by the hands,
   And will not let thee go.

Elizabeth Barrett Browning

From: Sonnets from the Portuguese

I thought once how Theocritus had sung
   Of the sweet years, the dear and wished-for years,
   Who each one in a gracious hand appears
To bear a gift for mortals, old or young:
And, as I mused it in his antique tongue,
   I saw, in gradual vision through my tears,
   The sweet, sad years, the melancholy years,
Those of my own life, who by turns had flung
A shadow across me. Straightway I was 'ware,
   So weeping, how a mystic Shape did move
Behind me, and drew me backward by the hair;
   And a voice said in mastery, while I strove, . . .
"Guess now who holds thee?" – "Death," I said. But there,
   The silver answer rang, . . . "Not Death, but Love."

What can I give thee back, O liberal
   And princely giver, who hast brought the gold
   And purple of thine heart, unstained, untold,
And laid them on the outside of the wall

For such as I to take or leave withal,
  In unexpected largesse? am I cold,
  Ungrateful, that for these most manifold
High gifts, I render nothing back at all?
Not so; not cold, — but very poor instead.
  Ask God who knows. For frequent tears have run
The colours from my life, and left so dead
  And pale a stuff, it were not fitly done
To give the same as pillow to thy head.
  Go farther! let it serve to trample on.

Yet love, mere love, is beautiful indeed
  And worthy of acceptation. Fire is bright,
  Let temple burn, or flax. An equal light
Leaps in the flame from cedar-plank or weed.
And love is fire; and when I say at need
  I love thee . . . mark! . . . I love thee! . . . in thy
  sight
  I stand transfigured, glorified aright,
With conscience of the new rays that proceed
Out of my face toward thine. There's nothing low
  In love, when love the lowest: meanest creatures
Who love God, God accepts while loving so.
  And what I feel, across the inferior features

Of what I am, doth flash itself, and show
  How that great work of Love enhances Nature's.

If thou must love me, let it be for naught
  Except for love's sake only. Do not say
  "I love her for her smile . . . her look . . . her way
Of speaking gently, . . . for a trick of thought
That falls in well with mine, and certes brought
  A sense of pleasant ease on such a day" –
  For these things in themselves, Belovèd, may
Be changed, or change for thee, – and love, so wrought,
May be unwrought so. Neither love me for
  Thine own dear pity's wiping my cheeks dry, –
A creature might forget to weep, who bore
  Thy comfort long, and lose thy love thereby!
But love me for love's sake, that evermore
  Thou mayst love on, through love's eternity.

How do I love thee? Let me count the ways.
  I love thee to the depth and breadth and height
  My soul can reach, when feeling out of sight
For the ends of Being and ideal Grace.
I love thee to the level of every day's
  Most quiet need, by sun and candlelight.

I love thee freely, as men strive for Right;
I love thee purely, as they turn from Praise.
I love thee with the passion put to use
    In my old griefs, and with my childhood's faith.
I love thee with a love I seemed to lose
    With my lost saints, — I love thee with the breath,
Smiles, tears, of all my life! — and, if God choose,
    I shall but love thee better after death.

ROBERT BROWNING

A WOMAN'S LAST WORD

Let's contend no more, Love,
Strive nor weep:
All be as before, Love,
— Only sleep!

What so wild as words are?
I and thou
In debate, as birds are,
Hawk on bough!

See the creature stalking
While we speak!
Hush and hide the talking,
Cheek on cheek!

What so false as truth is,
False to thee?
Where the serpent's tooth is,
Shun the tree —

Where the apple reddens
Never pry —
Lest we lose our Edens,
Eve and I.

Be a god and hold me
With a charm!
Be a man and fold me
With thine arm!

Teach me, only teach, Love!
As I ought
I will speak thy speech, Love,
Think thy thought —

Meet, if thou require it,
Both demands,
Laying flesh and spirit
In thy hands.

That shall be to-morrow
Not to-night:
I must bury sorrow
Out of sight:

— Must a little weep, Love,
(Foolish me!)
And so fall asleep, Love,
Loved by thee.

ROBERT BURNS

A RED, RED ROSE

O my Luve's like a red, red rose
That's newly sprung in June;
O my Luve's like the melodie
That's sweetly play'd in tune.

As fair art thou, my bonnie lass,
So deep in luve am I;
And I will luve thee still, my dear,
Till a' the seas gang dry.

Till a' the seas gang dry, my Dear,
And the rocks melt wi' the sun;
O I will love thee still, my dear,
While the sands o' life shall run.

And fare thee weel, my only Luve!
And fare thee weel a while!
And I will come again, my Luve,
Tho' it were ten thousand mile!

LORD BYRON

ALL FOR LOVE

O talk not to me of a name great in story;
The days of our youth are the days of our glory;
And the myrtle and ivy of sweet two-and-twenty
Are worth all your laurels, though ever so plenty.

What are garlands and crowns to the brow that is
*   wrinkled?*
'Tis but as a dead flower with May-dew besprinkled:
Then away with all such from the head that is hoary –
What care I for the wreaths that can only give glory?
O Fame! – if I e'er took delight in thy praises,
'Twas less for the sake of thy high-sounding phrases,
Than to see the bright eyes of the dear one discover
She thought that I was not unworthy to love her.

There chiefly I sought thee, there only I found thee;
Her glance was the best of the rays that surround thee;
When it sparkled o'er aught that was bright in my story,
I knew it was love, and I felt it was glory.

THOMAS CAMPBELL

THE MAID OF NEIDPATH

Earl March look'd on his dying child,
And, smit with grief to view her –
"The youth," he cried, "whom I exiled
Shall be restored to woo her."

She's at the window many an hour
His coming to discover:
And he look'd up to Ellen's bower
And she look'd on her lover –

But ah! so pale, he knew her not,
Though her smile on him was dwelling –
"And am I then forgot – forgot?"
It broke the heart of Ellen.

In vain he weeps, in vain he sighs,
Her cheek is cold as ashes;
Nor love's own kiss shall wake those eyes
To life their silken lashes.

THOMAS CAMPION

LOVE ME OR NOT

Love me or not, love her I must or die;
Leave me or not, follow her needs must I.
O that her grace would my wished comforts give.
How rich in her, how happy should I live!

All my desire, all my delight should be,
Her to enjoy, her to unite to me:
Envy should cease, her would I love alone:
Who loves by looks, is seldom true to one.

Could I enchant, and that it lawful were,
Her would I charm softly that none should hear.
But love enforced rarely yields firm content;
So would I love that neither should repent.

THOMAS CAMPION

THERE IS A GARDEN IN HER FACE

There is a garden in her face
   Where roses and white lilies grow;
A heavenly paradise is that place
   Wherein all pleasant fruits do flow.
There cherries grow which none may buy,
Till 'cherry-ripe' themselves do cry.

Those cherries fairly do enclose
   Of orient pearl a double row,
Which when her lovely laughter shows,
   They look like rosebuds filled with snow.
Yet them nor peer nor prince can buy,
Till 'cherry-ripe' themselves do cry.

Her eyes like angels watch them still,
   Her brows like bended bows do stand,
Threatening with piercing frowns to kill
   All that attempt, with eye or hand,
Those sacred cherries to come nigh,
Till 'cherry-ripe' themselves do cry.

THOMAS CAREW

BOLDNESS IN LOVE

Mark how the bashful morn in vain
   Courts the amorous marigold
With sighing blasts and weeping rain,
   Yet she refuses to unfold;
But when the planet of the day
Approacheth with his powerful ray
Then she spreads, then she receives
His warmer beams into her virgin leaves.

So shalt thou thrive in love, fond boy;
   If thy tears and sighs discover
Thy grief, thou never shalt enjoy
   The just reward of a bold lover.
But when with moving accents thou
Shalt constant faith and service vow,
Thy Celia shall receive those charms
With open ears, and with unfolded arms.

HENRY CAREY

SALLY IN OUR ALLEY

Of all the girls that are so smart
There's none like pretty Sally;
She is the darling of my heart,
And she lives in our alley.
There is no lady in the land
Is half so sweet as Sally;
She is the darling of my heart,
And she lives in our alley.

Her father he makes cabbage-nets
And through the street does cry 'em;
Her mother she sells laces long
To such as please to buy 'em:
But sure such folks could ne'er beget
So sweet a girl as Sally!
She is the darling of my heart,
And she lives in our alley.

When she is by, I leave my work,
I love her so sincerely;

My master comes like any Turk,
And bangs me most severely –
But let him bang his bellyful,
I'll bear it all for Sally;
She is the darling of my heart,
And she lives in our alley.

Of all the days that's in the week
I dearly love but one day –
And that's the day that comes betwixt
A Saturday and Monday;
For then I'm drest all in my best
To walk abroad with Sally;
She is the darling of my heart,
And she lives in our alley.

My master carries me to church,
And often am I blamed
Because I leave him in the lurch
As soon as text is named;
I leave the church in sermon-time
And slink away to Sally;
She is the darling of my heart,
And she lives in our alley.

When Christmas comes about again
O then I shall have money;
I'll hoard it up, and box and all,
I'll give it to my honey:
I would it were ten thousand pound,
I'd give it all to Sally;
She is the darling of my heart,
And she lives in our alley.

My master and the neighbours all
Make game of me and Sally,
And, but for her, I'd better be
A slave and row a galley;
But when my seven long years are out
O then I'll marry Sally, –
O then we'll wed, and then we'll bed,
But not in our alley!

HARTLEY COLERIDGE

SHE IS NOT FAIR TO OUTWARD VIEW

She is not fair to outward view
* As many maidens be;*
Her loveliness I never knew
* Until she smiled on me.*
O then I saw her eye was bright,
A well of love, a spring of light.

But now her looks are coy and cold,
* To mine they ne'er reply,*
And yet I cease not to behold
* The love-light in her eye:*
Her very frowns are fairer far
Than smiles of other maidens are.

SAMUEL TAYLOR COLERIDGE

LOVE

All thoughts, all passions, all delights,
Whatever stirs this mortal frame,
All are but ministers of Love,
*   And feed his sacred flame.*

Oft in my waking dreams do I
Live o'er again that happy hour,
When midway on the mount I lay
*   Beside the ruin'd tower.*

The moonshine stealing o'er the scene
Had blended with the lights of eve;
And she was there, my hope, my joy,
*   My own dear Genevieve!*

She lean'd against the arméd man,
The statue of the arméd knight;
She stood and listen'd to my lay,
*   Amid the lingering light.*

Few sorrows hath she of her own,
My hope! my joy! my Genevieve!
She loves me best whene'er I sing
    The songs that make her grieve.

I play'd a soft and doleful air,
I sang an old and moving story —
An old rude song, that suited well
    That ruin wild and hoary.

She listen'd with a flitting blush,
With downcast eyes and modest grace;
For well she knew I could not choose
    But gaze upon her face.

I told her of the Knight that wore
Upon his shield a burning brand;
And that for ten long years he woo'd
    The Lady of the Land.

I told her how he pined; and ah!
The deep, the low, the pleading tone
With which I sang another's love
    Interpreted my own.

She listen'd with a flitting blush,
With downcast eyes and modest grace;
And she forgave me, that I gazed
    Too fondly on her face.

But when I told the cruel scorn
That crazed that bold and lovely Knight,
And that he cross'd the mountain-woods,
    Nor rested day nor night;

That sometimes from the savage den,
And sometimes from the darksome shade,
And sometimes starting up at once
    In green and sunny glade

There came and look'd him in the face
An angel beautiful and bright;
And that he knew it was a Fiend,
    This miserable Knight!

And that, unknowing what he did,
He leap'd amid a murderous band,
And saved from outrage worse than death
    The Lady of the Land;

And how she wept, and clasp'd his knees
And how she tended him in vain;
And ever strove to expiate
  The scorn that crazed his brain;

And that she nursed him in a cave,
And how his madness went away,
When on the yellow forest leaves
  A dying man he lay;

– His dying words – but when I reach'd
That tenderest strain of all the ditty,
My faltering voice and pausing harp
  Disturb'd her soul with pity!

All impulses of soul and sense
Had thrill'd my guileless Genevieve;
The music and the doleful tale,
  The rich and balmy eve;

And hopes, and fears that kindle hope,
An undistinguishable throng,
And gentle wishes long subdued,
  Subdued and cherish'd long!

She wept with pity and delight,
She blush'd with love and virgin shame;
And like the murmur of a dream,
  I heard her breathe my name.

Her bosom heaved — she stepp'd aside,
As conscious of my look she stept —
Then suddenly, with timorous eye
  She fled to me and wept.

She half enclosed me with her arms,
She press'd me with a meek embrace;
And bending back her head, look'd up,
  And gazed upon my face.

'Twas partly love, and partly fear,
And partly 'twas a bashful art,
That I might rather feel, than see,
  The swelling of her heart.

I calm'd her fears, and she was calm,
And told her love with virgin pride;
And so I won my Genevieve,
  My bright and beauteous Bride.

HENRY CONSTABLE

MY LADY'S PRESENCE MAKES THE ROSES RED

My lady's presence makes the roses red,
Because to see her lips they blush for shame.
The lily's leaves, for envy, pale became,
And her white hands in them this envy bred.
The marigold the leaves abroad doth spread,
Because the sun's and her power is the same.
The violet of purple colour came,
Dyed in the blood she made my heart to shed.
In brief: all flowers from her their virtue take;
From her sweet breath their sweet smells do proceed;
The living heat which her eyebeams doth make
Warmeth the ground, and quickeneth the seed.
　　The rain, wherewith she watereth the flowers,
　　Falls from mine eyes, which she dissolves in showers.

WILLIAM COWPER

TO THE SAME

The twentieth year is well-nigh past
Since first our sky was overcast;
Ah, would that this might be the last!
    My Mary!

Thy spirits have a fainter flow,
I see thee daily weaker grow —
'Twas my distress that brought thee low,
    My Mary!

Thy needles, once a shining store,
For my sake restless heretofore,
Now rust disused, and shine no more;
    My Mary!

For though thou gladly wouldst fulfil
The same kind office for me still,
Thy sight now seconds not thy will,
    My Mary!

But well thou play'dst the housewife's part,
And all thy threads with magic art
Have wound themselves about this heart,
   My Mary!

Thy indistinct expressions seem
Like language utter'd in a dream;
Yet me they charm, whate'er the theme,
   My Mary!

Thy silver locks, once auburn bright,
Are still more lovely in my sight
Than golden beams of orient light,
   My Mary!

For could I view nor them nor thee,
What sight worth seeing could I see?
The sun would rise in vain for me,
   My Mary!

Partakers of thy sad decline
Thy hands their little force resign;
Yet, gently press'd, press gently mine,
   My Mary!

Such feebleness of limbs thou prov'st
That now at every step thou mov'st
Upheld by two; yet still thou lov'st,
   My Mary!

And still to love, though press'd with ill,
In wintry age to feel no chill,
With me is to be lovely still,
   My Mary!

But ah! by constant heed I know
How oft the sadness that I show
Transforms thy smiles to looks of woe,
   My Mary!

And should my future lot be cast
With much resemblance of the past,
Thy worn-out heart will break at last —
   My Mary!

GEORGE DARLEY

THE LOVELINESS OF LOVE

It is not Beauty I demand,
A crystal brow, the moon's despair,
Nor the snow's daughter, a white hand,
Nor mermaid's yellow pride of hair:

Tell me not of your starry eyes,
Your lips that seem on roses fed,
Your breasts, where Cupid trembling lies
Nor sleeps for kissing of his bed: –

A bloomy pair of vermeil cheeks
Like Hebe's in her ruddiest hours,
A breath that softer music speaks
Than summer winds a-wooing flowers,

These are but gauds: nay, what are lips?
Coral beneath the ocean-stream,
Whose brink when your adventurer sips
Full oft he perisheth on them.

And what are cheeks, but ensigns oft
That wave hot youth to fields of blood?
Did Helen's breast, though ne'er so soft,
Do Greece or Ilium any good?

Eyes can with baleful ardour burn;
Poison can breath, that erst perfumed;
There's many a white hand holds an urn
With lovers' hearts to dust consumed.

For crystal brows — there's nought within;
They are but empty cells for pride;
He who the Syren's hair would win
Is mostly strangled in the tide.

Give me, instead of Beauty's bust,
A tender heart, a loyal mind
Which with temptation I could trust,
Yet never link'd with error find, —

One in whose gentle bosom I
Could pour my secret heart of woes,
Like the care-burthen'd honey-fly
That hides his murmurs in the rose, —

My earthly Comforter! whose love
So indefeasible might be
That, when my spirit won above,
Hers could not stay, for sympathy.

JOHN DONNE

THE GOOD MORROW

I wonder by my troth, what thou and I
Did, till we loved? were we not weaned till then?
But sucked on country pleasures, childishly?
Or snorted we in the seven sleepers' den?
'Twas so; but this, all pleasures fancies be.
If ever any beauty I did see,
Which I desired, and got, 'twas but a dream of thee.

And now good-morrow to our waking souls,
Which watch not one another out of fear;
For love all love of other sights controls,
And makes one little room an everywhere.
Let sea-discoverers to new worlds have gone,
Let maps to other, worlds on worlds have shown,
Let us possess one world, each hath one, and is one.

My face in thine eye, thine in mine appears,
And true plain hearts do in the faces rest,
Where can we find two better hemispheres
Without sharp North, without declining West?
Whatever dies, was not mixed equally;
If our two loves be one, or thou and I
Love so alike that none do slacken, none can die.

JOHN DONNE

SONG

Go, and catch a falling star,
  Get with child a mandrake root,
Tell me, where all past years are,
  Or who cleft the Devil's foot,
Teach me to hear mermaids singing,
Or to keep off envy's stinging,
    And find
    What wind
Serves to advance an honest mind.

If thou beest born to strange sights,
  Things invisible to see,
Ride ten thousand days and nights
  Till age snow white hairs on thee,
Thou, when thou return'st wilt tell me
All strange wonders that befell thee,
    And swear
    No where
Lives a woman true, and fair.

If thou find'st one, let me know,
　　Such a pilgrimage were sweet;
Yet do not, I would not go,
　　Though at next door we might meet,
Though she were true, when you met her,
And last, till you write your letter,
　　　　Yet she
　　　　Will be
False, ere I come, to two, or three.

MICHAEL DRAYTON

LOVE'S FAREWELL

Since there's no help, come let us kiss and part, –
Nay I have done, you get no more of me;
And I am glad, yea, glad with all my heart,
That thus so cleanly I myself can free;

Shake hands for ever, cancel all our vows,
And when we meet at any time again,
Be it not seen in either of our brows
That we one jot of former love retain.

Now at the last gasp of love's latest breath,
When, his pulse failing, passion speechless lies,
When faith is kneeling by his bed of death,
And innocence is closing up his eyes,

– Now if thou would'st, when all have given him over,
From death to life thou might'st him yet recover!

JOHN FLETCHER

SONG

Do not fear to put thy feet
Naked in the river sweet;
Think not leech, or newt, or toad,
Will bite thy foot, when thou hast trod:
Nor let the water rising high,
As thou wad'st in, make thee cry
And sob; but ever live with me,
And not a wave shall trouble thee!

GEORGE GASCOIGNE

THE LOOKS OF A LOVER ENAMOURED

Thou, with thy looks, on whom I look full oft,
And find therein great cause of deep delight,
Thy face is fair, thy skin is smooth and soft,
Thy lips are sweet, thine eyes are clear and bright,
And every part seems pleasant in my sight;
Yet wote thou well, those looks have wrought my woe,
Because I love to look upon them so.

For first those looks allured mine eye to look,
And straight mine eye stirred up my heart to love;
And cruel love, with deep deceitful hook,
Choked up my mind, whom fancy cannot move,
Nor hope relieve, nor other help behoove
But still to look; and though I look too much,
Needs must I look because I see none such.

Thus in thy looks my love and life have hold;
And with such life my death draws on apace;
And for such death no med'cine can be told
But looking still upon thy lovely face,
Wherein are painted pity, peace, and grace.
Then though thy looks should cause me for to die,
Needs must I look, because I live thereby.

Since then thy looks my life have so in thrall
As I can like none other looks but thine,
Lo, here I yield my life, my love and all
Into thy hands, and all things else resign
But liberty to gaze upon thine eyen:
Which when I do, then think it were thy part
To look again, and link with me in heart.

Robert Herrick

To Anthea Who May Command Him Anything

Bid me to live, and I will live
Thy Protestant to be:
Or bid me love, and I will give
A loving heart to thee.

A heart as soft, a heart as kind,
A heart as sound and free
As in the whole world thou canst find,
That heart I'll give to thee.

Bid that heart stay, and it will stay,
To honour thy decree:
Or bid it languish quite away,
And 't shall do so for thee.

Bid me to weep, and I will weep
While I have eyes to see:
And, having none, yet I will keep
A heart to weep for thee.

Bid me despair, and I'll despair
Under that cypress tree:
Or bid me die, and I will dare
E'en Death, to die for thee.

Thou art my life, my love, my heart,
The very eyes of me,
And hast command of every part,
To live and die for thee.

ROBERT HERRICK
UPON JULIA'S CLOTHES

From Hesperides

When as in silks my Julia goes,
Then, then (me thinks) how sweetly flows
That liquefaction of her clothes.

Next, when I cast mine eyes and see
That brave vibration each way free;
O how that glittering taketh me!

LAURENCE HOPE

KASHMIRI SONG

Pale hands I loved beside the Shalimar,
Where are you now? Who lies beneath your spell?
Whom do you lead on Rapture's roadway, far,
Before you agonise them in farewell?
Pale hands I loved beside the Shalimar,
Where are you now? Where are you now?

Pale hands, pinked tipped, like Lotus buds that float
On those cool waters where we used to dwell,
I would have rather felt you round my throat
Crushing out life, than waving me farewell!
Pale hands I loved beside the Shalimar,
Where are you now? Where are you now?

A.E. HOUSMAN

BREDON HILL

In summertime on Bredon
  The bells they sound so clear;
Round both the shires they ring them
  In steeples far and near,
    A happy noise to hear.

Here of a Sunday morning
  My love and I would lie,
And see the coloured counties,
  And hear the larks so high
    About us in the sky.

The bells would ring to call her
  In valleys miles away:
"Come all to church, good people;
  Good people, come and pray."
    But here my love would stay.

And I would turn and answer
  Among the springing thyme,
"Oh, peal upon our wedding,
  And we will hear the chime,
  And come to church in time."

But when the snows at Christmas
  On Bredon top were strown,
My love rose up so early
  And stole out unbeknown
  And went to church alone.

They tolled the one bell only,
  Groom there was none to see,
The mourners followed after,
  And so to church went she,
  And would not wait for me.

The bells they sound on Bredon,
  And the steeples hum.
"Come all to church, good people, — "
  Oh, noisy bells, be dumb;
  I hear you, I will come.

Henry Howard, Earl of Surrey

Vow to Love Faithfully, Howsoever He be Rewarded

Set me whereas the sun doth parch the green,
Or where his beams do not dissolve the ice;
In temperate heat, where he is felt and seen;
In presence prest of people, mad, or wise;
Set me in high, or yet in low degree;
In longest night, or in the shortest day;
In clearest sky, or where clouds thickest be;
In lusty youth, or when my hairs are grey;
Set me in heaven, in earth, or else in hell,
In hill, or dale, or in the foaming flood;
Thrall, or at large, alive whereso I dwell,
Sick, or in health, in evil fame or good,
   Hers will I be; and only with this thought
   Content myself, although my chance be nought.

BEN JONSON

TO CELIA

Drink to me only with thine eyes,
And I will pledge with mine;
Or leave a kiss but in the cup
And I'll not look for wine.
The thirst that from the soul doth rise
Doth ask a drink divine;
But might I of Jove's nectar sup,
I would not change for thine.

I sent thee late a rosy wreath,
Not so much honouring thee
As giving it a hope that there
It could not wither'd be;
But thou thereon didst only breathe
And sent'st it back to me;
Since when it grows, and smells, I swear,
Not of itself but thee!

CHARLES KINGSLEY

AIRLY BEACON

Airly Beacon, Airly Beacon;
Oh the pleasant sight to see
Shires and towns from Airly Beacon,
While my love climbed up to me!

Airly Beacon, Airly Beacon;
Oh the happy hours we lay
Deep in fern on Airly Beacon,
Courting through the summer's day!

Airly Beacon, Airly Beacon;
Oh the weary haunt for me,
All alone on Airly Beacon,
With his baby on my knee!

Walter Savage Landor

The Maid's Lament

I loved him not; and yet now he is gone
  I feel I am alone.
I checked him while he spoke; yet could he speak,
  Alas! I would not check.
For reasons not to love him once I sought,
  And wearied all my thought
To vex myself and him: I now would give
  My love, could he but live
Who lately lived for me, and, when he found
  'Twas vain, in holy ground
He hid his face amid the shades of death.
  I waste for him my breath
Who wasted his for me: but mine returns,
  And this lorn bosom burns
With stifling heat, heaving it up in sleep,
  And waking me to weep
Tears that had melted his soft heart: for years
  Wept he bitter tears.
Merciful God! *such was his latest prayer,*
  These may she never share!

Quieter is his breath, his breast more cold,
  Than daisies in the mould,
Where children spell, athwart the churchyard gate,
  His name and life's brief date.
Pray for him, gentle souls, whoe'er you be,
  And, O, pray too for me!

RICHARD LOVELACE

TO ALTHEA FROM PRISON

When Love with unconfinèd wings
Hovers within my gates,
And my divine Althea brings
To whisper at the grates;
When I lie tangled in her hair
And fetter'd to her eye,
The Gods that wanton in the air
Know no such liberty.

When flowing cups run swiftly round
With no allaying Thames,
Our careless heads with roses crown'd,
Our hearts with loyal flames;
When thirsty grief in wine we steep,
When healths and draughts go free –
Fishes that tipple in the deep
Know no such liberty.

When, like committed linnets, I
With shriller throat shall sing
The sweetness, mercy, majesty
And glories of my King;
When I shall voice aloud how good
He is, how great should be,
Enlargéd winds, that curl the flood,
Know no such liberty.

Stone walls do not a prison make,
Nor iron bars a cage;
Minds innocent and quiet take
That for an hermitage:
If I have freedom in my love
And in my soul am free,
Angels alone, that soar above,
Enjoy such liberty.

JOHN LYLY

CUPID AND CAMPASPE

Cupid and my Campaspe play'd
At cards for kisses; Cupid paid:
He stakes his quiver, bow, and arrows,
His mother's doves, and team of sparrows;
Loses them too; then down he throws
The coral of his lips, the rose
Growing on's cheek (but none knows how);
With these, the crystal of his brow,
And then the dimple on his chin;
All these did my Campaspe win:
At last he set her both his eyes –
She won, and Cupid blind did rise.
O Love! has she done this to thee?
What shall, alas! become of me?

CHRISTOPHER MARLOWE

THE PASSIONATE SHEPHERD TO HIS LOVE

Come live with me and be my Love,
And we will all the pleasures prove
That hills and valleys, dale and field,
And all the craggy mountains yield.

There will we sit upon the rocks
And see the shepherds feed their flocks,
By shallow rivers, to whose falls
Melodious birds sing madrigals.

There will I make thee beds of roses
And a thousand fragrant posies,
A cap of flowers, and a kirtle
Embroider'd all with leaves of myrtle.

A gown made of the finest wool,
Which from our pretty lambs we pull,
Fair linéd slippers for the cold,
With buckles of the purest gold.

A belt of straw and ivy buds
With coral clasps and amber studs:
And if these pleasures may thee move,
Come live with me and be my Love.

Thy silver dishes for thy meat
As precious as the gods do eat,
Shall on an ivory table be
Prepared each day for thee and me.

The shepherd swains shall dance and sing
For thy delight each May-morning:
If these delights thy mind may move,
Then live with me and be my Love.

Sir Walter Raleigh

Her Reply

If all the world and love were young,
And truth in every shepherd's tongue,
These pretty pleasures might me move
To live with thee and be thy Love.

But Time drives flocks from field to fold;
When rivers rage and rocks grow cold;
And Philomel becometh dumb;
The rest complains of cares to come.

The flowers do fade, and wanton fields
To wayward Winter reckoning yields:
A honey tongue, a heart of gall,
Is fancy's spring, but sorrow's fall.

Thy gowns, thy shoes, thy beds of roses,
Thy cap, thy kirtle, and thy posies,
Soon break, soon wither – soon forgotten,
In folly ripe, in reason rotten.

Thy belt of straw and ivy-buds,
Thy coral clasps and amber studs, —
All these in me no means can move
To come to thee and be thy Love.

But could youth last, and love still breed,
Had joys no date, nor age no need,
Then these delights my mind might move
To live with thee and be thy Love.

ANDREW MARVELL

TO HIS COY MISTRESS

Had we but world enough, and time,
This coyness, Lady, were no crime.
We would sit down, and think which way
To walk, and pass our long love's day.
Thou by the Indian Ganges' side
Shouldst rubies find: I by the tide
Of Humber would complain. I would
Love you ten years before the Flood:
And you should, if you please, refuse
Till the conversion of the Jews.
My vegetable love should grow
Vaster than empires, and more slow.
An hundred years should go to praise
Thine eyes, and on thy forehead gaze.
Two hundred to adore each breast:
But thirty thousand to the rest.
An age at least to every part,
And the last age should show your heart.
For, Lady, you deserve this state;
Nor would I love at lower rate.
    But at my back I always hear
Time's wingèd chariot hurrying near:

And yonder all before us lie
Deserts of vast eternity.
Thy beauty shall no more be found;
Nor, in thy marble vault, shall sound
My echoing song: then worms shall try
That long preserved virginity:
And your quaint honour turn to dust;
And into ashes all my lust.
The grave's a fine and private place,
But none I think do there embrace.

   Now therefore, while the youthful hue
Sits on thy skin like morning dew,
And while thy willing soul transpires
At every pore with instant fires,
Now let us sport us while we may;
And now, like amorous birds of prey,
Rather at once our time devour,
Than languish in his slow-chapt power.
Let us roll all our strength, and all
Our sweetness, up into one ball:
And tear our pleasure with rough strife,
Thorough the iron gates of life.
Thus, though we cannot make our sun
Stand still, yet we will make him run.

GEORGE MEREDITH

FROM: MODERN LOVE

In our old shipwrecked days there was an hour,
When in the firelight steadily aglow,
Joined slackly, we beheld the red chasm grow
Among the clicking coals. Our library-bower
That eve was left to us: and hushed we sat
As lovers to whom Time is whispering.
From sudden-opened doors we heard them sing:
The nodding elders mixed good wine with chat.
Well knew we that Life's greatest treasure lay
With us, and of it was our talk. "Ah, yes!
Love dies!" I said: I never thought it less.
She yearned to me that sentence to unsay.
Then when the fire domed blackening, I found
Her cheek was salt against my kiss, and swift
Up the sharp scale of sobs her breast did lift: —
Now am I haunted by that taste! that sound!

Mark where the pressing wind shoots javelin-like
Its skeleton shadow on the broad-backed wave!
Here is a fitting spot to dig Love's grave;
Here where the ponderous breakers plunge and strike,

And dart their hissing tongues high up the sand:
In hearing of the ocean, and in sight
Of those ribbed wind-streaks running into white.
If I the death of Love had deeply planned,
I never could have made it half so sure,
As by the unblest kisses which upbraid
The full-waked sense; or failing that, degrade!
'Tis morning: but no morning can restore
What we have forfeited. I see no sin:
The wrong is mixed. In tragic life, God wot,
No villain need be! Passions spin the plot:
We are betrayed by what is false within.

We saw the swallows gathering in the sky,
And in the osier-isle we heard them noise.
We had not to look back on summer joys,
Or forward to a summer of bright dye:
But in the largeness of the evening earth
Our spirits grew as we went side by side.
The hour became her husband and my bride.
Love, that had robbed us so, thus blessed our dearth!
The pilgrims of the year waxed very loud
In multitudinous chatterings, as the flood
Full brown came from the West, and like pale blood

Expanded to the upper crimson cloud.
Love, that had robbed us of immortal things,
This little moment mercifully gave,
Where I have seen across the twilight wave
The swan sail with her young beneath her wings.

Thus piteously Love closed what he begat:
The union of this ever-diverse pair!
These two were rapid falcons in a snare,
Condemned to do the flitting of the bat.
Lovers beneath the singing sky of May,
They wandered once; clear as the dew on flowers:
But they fed not on the advancing hours:
Their hearts held cravings for the buried day.
Then each applied to each that fatal knife,
Deep questioning, which probes to endless dole.
Ah, what a dusty answer gets the soul
When hot for certainties in this our life! —
In tragic hints here see what evermore
Moves dark as yonder midnight ocean's force,
Thundering like ramping hosts of warrior horse,
To throw that faint thin line upon the shore!

WILLIAM JULIUS MICKLE
THE SAILOR'S WIFE

And are ye sure the news is true?
And are ye sure he's weel?
Is this a time to think o' wark?
Ye jades, lay by your wheel;
Is this the time to spin a thread,
When Colin's at the door?
Reach down my cloak, I'll to the quay,
And see him come ashore.
For there's nae luck about the house,
There's nae luck at a';
There's little pleasure in the house
When our gudeman's awa'.

And gie to me my bigonet,
My bishop's satin gown;
For I maun tell the baillie's wife
That Colin's in the town.
My Turkey slippers maun gae on,
My stockins pearly blue;
It's a' to pleasure our gudeman,
For he's baith leal and true.

Rise, lass, and mak a clean fireside,
Put on the muckle pot;
Gie little Kate her button gown
And Jock his Sunday coat;
And mak their shoon as black as slaes,
Their hose as white as snaw;
It's a' to please my ain gudeman,
For he's been long awa'.

There's twa fat hens upo' the coop
Been fed this month and mair;
Mak haste and thraw their necks about,
That Colin weel may fare;
And spread the table neat and clean,
Gar ilka thing look braw,
For wha can tell how Colin fared
When he was far awa'?

Sae true his heart, sae smooth his speech,
His breath like caller air;
His very foot has music in't
As he comes up the stair –
And will I see his face again?
And will I hear him speak?

I'm downright dizzy wi' the thought,
In troth I'm like to greet!

If Colin's weel, and weel content,
I hae nae mair to crave:
And gin I live to keep him sae,
I'm blest aboon the lave:
And will I see his face again,
And will I hear him speak?
I'm downright dizzy wi' the thought,
In troth I'm like to greet.
For there's nae luck about the house,
There's nae luck at a';
There's little pleasure in the house
When our gudeman's awa'.

THOMAS MOORE

AT THE MID HOUR OF NIGHT . . .

At the mid hour of night, when stars are weeping, I fly
To the lone vale we loved, when life shone warm in thine
    eye;
And I think oft, if spirits can steal from the regions of air
To revisit past scenes of delight, thou wilt come to me
    there
And tell me our love is remember'd, even in the sky!

Then I sing the wild song it once was rapture to hear
When our voices, commingling, breathed like one on the
    ear;
And as Echo far off through the vale my sad orison rolls,
I think, O my Love! 'tis thy voice, from the Kingdom of
    Souls
Faintly answering still the notes that once were so dear.

CAROLINE E.S. NORTON

I DO NOT LOVE THEE! . . .

I do not love thee! – no! I do not love thee!
And yet when thou art absent I am sad;
And envy even the bright blue sky above thee,
Whose quiet stars may see thee and be glad.

I do not love thee! – yet, I know not why,
Whate'er thou dost seems still well done, to me:
And often in my solitude I sigh
That those I do love are not more like thee!

I do not love thee! – yet, when thou art gone,
I hate the sound (though those who speak be dear)
Which breaks the lingering echo of the tone
Thy voice of music leaves upon my ear.

I do not love thee! – yet thy speaking eyes,
With their deep, bright, and most expressive blue,
Between me and the midnight heaven arise,
Oftener then any eyes I ever knew.

I know I do not love thee! yet, alas!
Others will scarcely trust my candid heart;
And oft I catch them smiling as they pass,
Because they see me gazing where thou art.

DAVID'S LAMENT

FROM: THE SECOND BOOK OF SAMUEL

*And David lamented with this lamentation over Saul and
over Jonathan his son:*

The beauty of Israel is slain upon thy high places:

How are the mighty fallen!

Tell it not in Gath,

Publish it not in the streets of Askelon;

Lest the daughters of the Philistines rejoice,

Lest the daughters of the uncircumcised triumph.

Ye mountains of Gilboa,

Let there be no dew, neither let there be rain, upon
*   you, nor fields of offerings:*

For there the shield of the mighty is vilely cast away,

The shield of Saul, as though he had not been
*   anointed with oil.*

From the blood of the slain, from the fat of the mighty,

The bow of Jonathan turned not back,

And the sword of Saul returned not empty.

Saul and Jonathan were lovely and pleasant in their
*   lives,*

And in their death they were not divided:

They were swifter than eagles,

They were stronger than lions.
Ye daughters of Israel, weep over Saul,
Who clothed you in scarlet, with other delights,
Who put on ornaments of gold upon your apparel.
How are the mighty fallen in the midst of the battle!
O Jonathan, thou wast slain in thine high places.
I am distressed for thee, my brother Jonathan:
Very pleasant hast thou been unto me:
Thy love to me was wonderful,
Passing the love of women.
How are the mighty fallen,
And the weapons of war perished!

FROM: THE SONG OF SOLOMON

2 *I am the rose of Sharon,*
  And the lily of the valleys.

  As the lily among thorns,
  So is my love among the daughters.

  As the apple tree among the trees of the wood,
  So is my beloved among the sons.
  I sat down under his shadow with great delight,
  And his fruit was sweet to my taste.
  He brought me to the banqueting house,
  And his banner over me was love.
  Stay me with flagons, comfort me with apples:
  For I am sick of love.
  His left hand is under my head,
  And his right hand doth embrace me.
  I charge you, O ye daughters of Jerusalem,
  By the roes, and by the hinds of the field,
  That ye stir not up, nor awake my love,
  Till he please.

The voice of my beloved! behold, he cometh
Leaping upon the mountains, skipping upon the hills.
My beloved is like a roe or a young hart:
Behold, he standeth behind our wall,
He looketh forth at the windows,
Shewing himself through the lattice.

My beloved spake, and said unto me,
Rise up, my love, my fair one, and come away.
For, lo, the winter is past,
The rain is over and gone;
The flowers appear on the earth;
The time of the singing of birds is come,
And the voice of the turtle is heard in our land;
The fig tree putteth forth her green figs,
And the vines with the tender grape
Give a good smell.
Arise, my love, my fair one, and come away.
O my dove, that art in the clefts of the rock, in the secret
* places of the stairs,*
Let me see thy countenance, let me hear thy voice;
For sweet is thy voice, and thy countenance is comely.

Take us the foxes, the little foxes, that spoil the vines:
For our vines have tender grapes.
My beloved is mine, and I am his:
He feedeth among the lilies.
Until the day break, and the shadows flee away,
Turn, my beloved, and be thou like a roe or a young
  hart
Upon the mountains of Bether.

3 *By night on my bed I sought him whom my soul*
  loveth:
I sought him, but I found him not.
I will rise now, and go about the city
In the streets, and in the broad ways
I will seek him whom my soul loveth:
I sought him, but I found him not.
The watchmen that go about the city found me:
To whom I said, Saw ye him whom my soul loveth?
It was but a little that I passed from them,
But I found him whom my soul loveth:
I held him and would not let him go,
Until I had brought him into my mother's house,
And into the chamber of her that conceived me.

I charge you, O ye daughters of Jerusalem,
By the roes, and by the hinds of the field,
That ye stir not up, nor awake my love,
Till he please.

*   *   *

4 *Behold, thou art fair, my love; behold, thou art fair;*
Thou hast doves' eyes within thy locks:
Thy hair is as a flock of goats,
That appear from mount Gilead.
Thy teeth are like a flock of sheep that are even shorn,
Which came up from the washing;
Whereof every one bear twins,
And none is barren among them.
Thy lips are like a thread of scarlet,
And thy speech is comely:
Thy temples are like a piece of a pomegranate
Within thy locks.
Thy neck is like the tower of David builded for an
    armoury,
Whereon there hang a thousand bucklers,
All shields of mighty men.
Thy two breasts are like two young roes that are twins,
Which feed among the lilies.

Until the day break, and the shadows flee away,
I will get me to the mountain of myrrh,
And to the hill of frankincense.
Thou art all fair, my love;
There is no spot in thee.
Come with me from Lebanon, my spouse,
With me from Lebanon:
Look from the top of Amana,
From the top of Shenir and Hermon,
From the lions' dens,
From the mountains of the leopards.
Thou hast ravished my heart, my sister, my spouse;
Thou hast ravished my heart with one of thine eyes,
With one chain of thy neck.
How fair is thy love, my sister, my spouse!
How much better is thy love than wine!
And the smell of thine ointments than all spices!
Thy lips, O my spouse, drop as the honeycomb:
Honey and milk are under thy tongue;
And the smell of thy garments is like the smell of
    Lebanon.
A garden inclosed is my sister, my spouse;
A spring shut up, a fountain sealed.
Thy plants are an orchard of pomegranates, with
    pleasant fruits;

Camphire, with spikenard,
Spikenard and saffron;
Calamus and cinnamon, with all trees of frankincense;
Myrrh and aloes, with all the chief spices:
A fountain of gardens,
A well of living waters,
And streams from Lebanon.

Awake, O north wind; and come, thou south;
Blow upon my garden, that the spices thereof may flow
    out.
Let my beloved come into his garden,
And eat his pleasant fruits.

Thomas Love Peacock

The Grave of Love

I dug, beneath the cypress shade,
What well might seem an elfin's grave;
And every pledge in earth I laid,
That erst thy false affection gave.

I pressed them down the sod beneath;
I placed one mossy stone above;
And twined the rose's fading wreath
Around the sepulchre of love.

Frail as thy love, the flowers were dead,
Ere yet the evening sun was set:
But years shall see the cypress spread,
Immutable as my regret.

JOSEPHINE V. ROWE

MACUSHLA

Macushla! Macushla! your sweet voice is calling,
Calling me softly again and again.
Macushla! Macushla! I hear its dear pleading,
My blue-eyed Macushla, I hear it in vain.

Macushla! Macushla! your white arms are reaching,
I feel their enfolding caressing me still.
Fling them out from the darkness, my lost love,
  Macushla,
Let them find me and bind me again if they will.

Macushla! Macushla! your red lips are saying
That death is a dream, and love is for aye.
Then awaken, Macushla, awake from your dreaming
My blue-eyed Macushla, awaken to stay.

SIR WALTER SCOTT

THE MAID OF NEIDPATH

O lovers' eyes are sharp to see,
And lovers' ears in hearing;
And love, in life's extremity,
Can lend an hour of cheering.
Disease had been in Mary's bower
And slow decay from mourning,
Though now she sits on Neidpath's tower
To watch her love's returning.

All sunk and dim her eyes so bright,
Her form decay'd by pining,
Till through her wasted hand, at night,
You saw the taper shining.
By fits a sultry hectic hue
Across her cheek was flying;
By fits so ashy pale she grew
Her maidens thought her dying.

Yet keenest powers to see and hear
Seem'd in her frame residing;
Before the watch-dog prick'd his ear
She heard her lover's riding;
Ere scarce a distant form was kenn'd
She knew and waved to greet him,
And o'er the battlement did bend
As on the wing to meet him.

He came – he pass'd – an heedless gaze,
As o'er some stranger glancing;
Her welcome, spoke in faltering phrase,
Lost in his courser's prancing –
The castle-arch, whose hollow tone
Returns each whisper spoken,
Could scarcely catch the feeble moan
Which told her heart was broken.

WILLIAM SHAKESPEARE

SONNET XVIII

Shall I compare thee to a summer's day?
Thou art more lovely and more temperate:
Rough winds do shake the darling buds of May,
And summer's lease hath all too short a date:
Sometime too hot the eye of heaven shines,
And often is his gold complexion dimmed:
And every fair from fair sometime declines,
By chance, or nature's changing course, untrimmed.
But thy eternal summer shall not fade,
Nor lose possession of that fair thou ow'st,
Nor shall death brag thou wander'st in his shade,
When in eternal lines to time thou grow'st;
   So long as men can breathe, or eyes can see,
   So long lives this, and this gives life to thee.

WILLIAM SHAKESPEARE

SONNET CXVI

Let me not to the marriage of true minds
Admit impediments: love is not love
Which alters when it alteration finds,
Or bends with the remover to remove.
Oh no! it is an ever-fixëd mark
That looks on tempests, and is never shaken;
It is the star to every wandering bark,
Whose worth's unknown, although his height be taken.
Love's not Time's fool, though rosy lips and cheeks
Within his bending sickle's compass come;
Love alters not with his brief hours and weeks,
But bears it out even to the edge of doom:
    If this be error, and upon me proved,
    I never writ, nor no man ever loved.

WILLIAM SHAKESPEARE

SONNET XXXIII

Full many a glorious morning have I seen
Flatter the mountain-tops with sovereign eye,
Kissing with golden face the meadows green,
Gilding pale streams with heavenly alchemy;
Anon permit the basest clouds to ride
With ugly rack on his celestial face,
And from the forlorn world his visage hide,
Stealing unseen to west with this disgrace:
Even so my sun one early morn did shine
With all-triumphant splendour on my brow;
But out, alack! he was but one hour mine;
The region cloud hath masked him from me now.
   Yet him for this my love no whit disdaineth;
   Suns of the world may stain when heaven's sun
     staineth.

WILLIAM SHAKESPEARE

SONNET LXXI

No longer mourn for me, when I am dead,
Than you shall hear the surly sullen bell
Give warning to the world that I am fled
From this vile world, with vilest worms to dwell;
Nay, if you read this line, remember not
The hand that writ it, for I love you so
That I in your sweet thoughts would be forgot,
If thinking on me then should make you woe.
Oh, if, I say, you look upon this verse
When I perhaps compounded am with clay,
Do not so much as my poor name rehearse,
But let your love even with my life decay;
*   Lest the wise world should look into your moan,*
*   And mock you with me after I am gone.*

PERCY BYSSHE SHELLEY

LOVE'S PHILOSOPHY

The fountains mingle with the river
And the rivers with the ocean,
The winds of heaven mix for ever
With a sweet emotion;
Nothing in the world is single,
All things by a law divine
In one another's being mingle –
Why not I with thine?

See the mountains kiss high heaven
And the waves clasp one another;
No sister-flower would be forgiven
If it disdain'd its brother:
And the sunlight clasps the earth,
And the moonbeams kiss the sea –
What are all these kissings worth
If thou kiss not me?

PERCY BYSSHE SHELLEY

TO HARRIET [SHELLEY]

Thy look of love has power to calm
The stormiest passion of my soul;
Thy gentle words are drops of balm
In life's too bitter bowl;
No grief is mine, but that alone
These choicest blessings I have known.

Harriet! if all who long to live
In the warm sunshine of thine eye,
That price beyond all pain must give, —
Beneath thy scorn to die;
Then hear thy chosen own too late
His heart most worthy of thy hate.

Be thou, then, one among mankind
Whose heart is harder not for state,
Thou only virtuous, gentle, kind
Amid a world of hate;
And by a slight endurance seal
A fellow-being's lasting weal.

For pale with anguish is his cheek,
His breath comes fast, his eyes are dim,
Thy name is struggling ere he speak,
Weak is each trembling limb;
In mercy let him not endure
The misery of a fatal cure.

Oh, trust for once no erring guide!
Bid the remorseless feeling flee;
'Tis malice, 'tis revenge, 'tis pride,
'Tis anything but thee;
Oh, deign a nobler pride to prove,
And pity if thou canst not love.

EDMUND SPENSER

ONE DAY I WROTE her NAME upon the STRAND

One day I wrote her name upon the strand,
But came the waves and washëd it away:
Again I wrote it with a second hand,
But came the tide and made my pains his prey.
"Vain man," said she, "that dost in vain essay
A mortal thing so to immortalise;
For I myself shall like to this decay,
And eke my name be wipëd out likewise."
"Not so," quod I, "let baser things devise
To die in dust, but you shall live by fame;
My verse your virtues rare shall èternise,
And in the heavens write your glorious name:
   Where, whenas Death shall all the world subdue,
   Our love shall live, and later life renew."

Sir John Suckling

Encouragements to a Lover

Why so pale and wan, fond lover?
  Prythee, why so pale?
Will, when looking well can't move her,
  Looking ill prevail?
  Prythee, why so pale?

Why so dull and mute, young sinner?
  Prythee, why so mute?
Will, when speaking well can't win her,
  Saying nothing do't?
  Prythee, why so mute?

Quit, quit, for shame! this will not move,
  This cannot take her;
If of herself she will not love,
  Nothing can make her:
  The devil take her!

ALFRED, LORD TENNYSON

BREAK, BREAK, BREAK

Break, break, break,
On thy cold grey stones, O Sea!
And I would that my tongue could utter
The thoughts that arise in me.

O well for the fisherman's boy,
That he shouts with his sister at play!
O well for the sailor lad,
That he sings in his boat on the bay!

And the stately ships go on
To their haven under the hill;
But O for the touch of a vanish'd hand,
And the sound of a voice that is still!

Break, break, break,
At the foot of thy crags, O Sea!
But the tender grace of a day that is dead
Will never come back to me.

GEORGE TURBERVILLE

TO HIS RING, GIVEN TO HIS LADY, WHEREIN WAS GRAVEN THIS VERSE, 'MY HEART IS YOURS'

Though thou, my ring, be small,
And slender be thy price,
Yet hast thou in thy compass couched
A lover's true device;
And though no ruby red,
Ne turquoise, trim thy top,
Nor other jewel that commends
The golden Vulcan's shop;
Yet may'st thou boldly vaunt,
And make a true report
For me that am thy master yet,
In such a semblant sort,
That aye 'my heart is hers';
Of thee I ask no more;
My pen and I will show the rest
Which yet I keep in store.
Be mindful of thy charge,
And of thy master's case:
Forget not that 'my heart is hers'

Though I be not in place.
When thou hast told thy tale
Which is but short and sweet,
Then let my Love conject the rest
Till she and I do meet.
For as 'my heart is hers',
So shall it be for aye:
My heart, my hand, my life, my limbs,
Are hers till dying day.
Yea, when the spirit gives up
And body breathes his last,
Say naytheless 'my heart is hers'
When life and all is past.

EDMUND WALLER

SONG

Go, lovely Rose –
Tell her that wastes her time and me,
    That now she knows,
When I resemble her to thee,
How sweet and fair she seems to be.

    Tell her that's young,
And shuns to have her graces spied,
    That hadst thou sprung
In deserts where no men abide,
Thou must have uncommended died.

    Small is the worth
Of beauty from the light retired:
    Bid her come forth,
Suffer herself to be desired,
And not blush so to be admired.

    Then die – that she
The common fate of all things rare
    May read in thee;
How small a part of time they share
That are so wondrous sweet and fair!

Fred E. Weatherly

Friend o' Mine

When you are happy, friend o' mine,
And all your skies are blue,
Tell me your luck, your fortune fine,
And let me laugh with you.
Tell me the hopes that spur you on,
The deeds you mean to do,
The gold you've struck, the fame you've won,
And let me joy – with you!

When you are sad and heart a-cold,
And all your skies are dark,
Tell me the dreams that mock'd your hold,
The shafts that miss'd the mark.
Am I not yours for weal or woe?
How else can friends prove true?
Tell me what breaks and brings you low,
And let me stand – with you!

So, when the night falls tremulous,
When the last lamp burns low,
And one of us or both of us
The long, lone road must go,
Look with your dear old eyes in mine,
Give me a handshake true;
Whatever fate our souls await
Let me be there — with you!

JOHN WILMOT, EARL OF ROCHESTER

THE MISTRESS

An age in her embraces passed
Would seem a winter's day,
Where life and light with envious haste
Are torn and snatched away.

But oh, how slowly minutes roll
When absent from her eyes,
That feed my love, which is my soul:
It languishes and dies.

For then no more a soul, but shade,
It mournfully does move
And haunts my breast, by absence made
The living tomb of love.

You wiser men, despise me not
Whose lovesick fancy raves
On shades of souls, and heaven knows what:
Short ages live in graves.

Whene'er those wounding eyes, so full
Of sweetness, you did see,
Had you not been profoundly dull,
You have gone mad like me.

Nor censure us, you who perceive
My best beloved and me
Sigh and lament, complain and grieve:
You think we disagree.

Alas! 'tis sacred jealousy,
Love raised to an extreme:
The only proof 'twixt her and me
We love, and do not dream.

Fantastic fancies fondly move
And in frail joys believe,
Taking false pleasure for true love;
But pain can ne'er deceive.

Kind jealous doubts, tormenting fears,
And anxious cares, when past,
Prove our hearts' treasure fixed and dear,
And make us blest at last.

WILLIAM WORDSWORTH

THE LOST LOVE

She dwelt among the untrodden ways
Beside the springs of Dove;
A maid whom there were none to praise,
And very few to love:

A violet by a mossy stone
Half hidden from the eye!
— Fair as a star, when only one
Is shining in the sky.

She lived unknown, and few could know
When Lucy ceased to be;
But she is in her grave, and oh,
The difference to me!

SIR THOMAS WYATT

THE LOVER'S APPEAL

And wilt thou leave me thus?
Say nay, say nay, for shame!
To save thee from the blame
Of all my grief and grame.
And wilt thou leave me thus?
Say nay! say nay!

And wilt thou leave me thus,
That hath loved thee so long
In wealth and woe among?
And is thy heart so strong
As for to leave me thus?
Say nay! say nay!

And wilt thou leave me thus,
That hath given thee my heart
Never for to depart
Neither for pain nor smart:
And wilt thou leave me thus?
Say nay! say nay!

And wilt thou leave me thus,
And have no more pity
Of him that loveth thee?
Alas, thy cruelty!
And wilt thou leave me thus?
Say nay! say nay!

SIR THOMAS WYATT

THE LOVER SHOWETH HOW HE IS FORSAKEN OF SUCH AS HE SOMETIME ENJOYED

They flee from me that sometime did me seek,
  With naked foot stalking within my chamber:
Once have I seen them gently, tame, and meek,
  That now are wild, and do not once remember
That sometime they have put themselves in danger
To take bread at my hand: and now they range,
  Busily seeking in continual change.

Thankèd be fortune, it hath been otherwise
  Twenty times better; but once espećial,
In thin array, after a pleasant guise,
  When her loose gown did from her shoulders fall,
And she me caught in her arms long and small,
And therewithal so sweetly did me kiss,
  And softly said, "Dear heart, how like you this?"

It was no dream; for I lay broad awaking:
   But all is turned now, through my gentleness,
Into a bitter fashion of forsaking;
   And I have leave to go of her goodnèss;
And she also to use new-fangleness.
But since that I unkindly so am served,
   "How like you this?" – what hath she now deserved?